TH!NK
JOURNAL

FROM TH!NK FC

Copyright © 2025 by THINK FC.

All rights reserved. This book or any portion thereof may not be reproduced or used in any manner whatsoever without the publisher's express written permission, except for brief quotations in a book review.

Published in the United Kingdom by

Coalville C.A.N. Community Publishing
Memorial Square,
Coalville,
Leicestershire,
England
LE67 3TU

First Published in 2025

ISBN 979-8316076598

TH!NK FC

"We don't fix communities or people; we share ways to recognize and value the strengths and qualities within the community and its people, finding ways to celebrate together."

Our aim is to level the playing field by sharing tools and resources to help others TH!NK differently, supporting people to make a difference personally and within their communities.

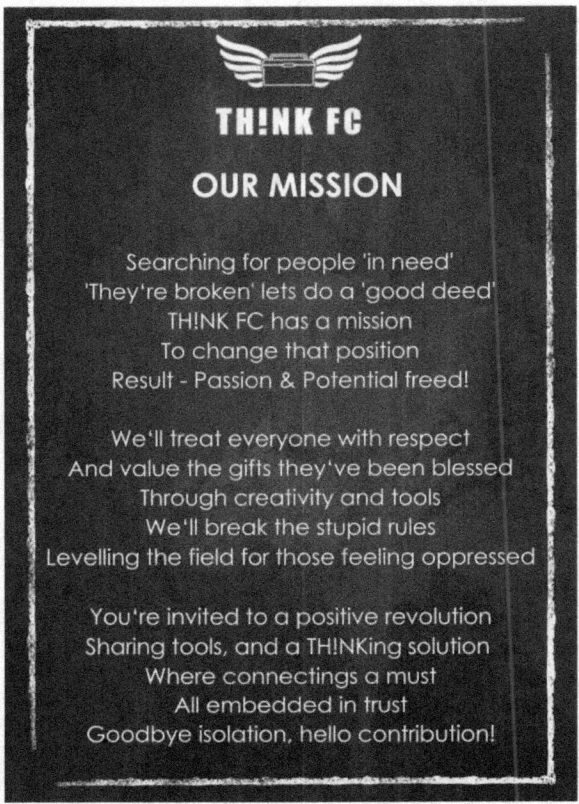

TH!NK FC

OUR MISSION

Searching for people 'in need'
'They're broken' lets do a 'good deed'
TH!NK FC has a mission
To change that position
Result - Passion & Potential freed!

We'll treat everyone with respect
And value the gifts they've been blessed
Through creativity and tools
We'll break the stupid rules
Levelling the field for those feeling oppressed

You're invited to a positive revolution
Sharing tools, and a TH!NKing solution
Where connectings a must
All embedded in trust
Goodbye isolation, hello contribution!

Check out our website for more tools and resources!
www.thinkfc.org.uk

Contents

Welcome to Your Journal. This is for you and your journey. The tools and resources shared here are to help with everyday life, making decisions and achieving goals that you set for yourself, celebrating along the way.

This Journal is yours for writing, drawing, doodling, whatever you want. There are no right or wrong answers and no expectations to share with anyone. Do whatever works for you.

Take your time - Happy TH!NKing!

Chapter 1 - ALL ABOUT ME
This chapter is all about you and is a chance to tell your story. TH!NK about where you have come from, where you are going and what you might want to do.

Chapter 2 - STRENGTHS AND SKILLS
This chapter gives you a chance to discover your individual strengths and skills. A place to TH!NK about the things you care about the most, what you are willing to do for yourself and in your community and how to connect.

Chapter 3 - GOAL SETTING AND TAKING ACTION
This chapter is about making it happen, taking action on things you care about most. There are lots of tools and resources here to help you on your journey to take the actions needed to achieve your goals.

NOTES

"Have fun - to be silly is to be human." Camerados

CHAPTER ONE

ALL ABOUT ME

All About Me

Reflect on Your Story so far

TH!NK about how you spend Your Time

Draw More About You

Pause to consider a Gratefulness Log

Who are the People in My Life and their influence

Try your hand at Letters From Me

Turn your Hindering Thoughts to Helpful Thoughts with the What Could I Bird

Pause for a Feelings Check In

Consider your Reasons Why

Connect with what matters to you in Your Life and your Good Life

Your Story

TH!NK about your journey in life so far. What is your story and what brought you here?

Use the space below to draw or write your story.
Have fun with it!

NOTES

"The more powerful the person you meet, the more surprising it is to find out they're making it up just like the rest of us."
Sam Coniff

Your Time

Have a TH!NK about how you spend your time in a typical week. What does your week ahead look like? Note down the things that you do.

What do you do for yourself?
What do you do for others?
What do you do for your community?

Monday

Tuesday

Wednesday

Thursday

Friday

Weekends

TH!NK about the things you've noted down in your typical week and plot them on the scale of enjoyability and usefulness.

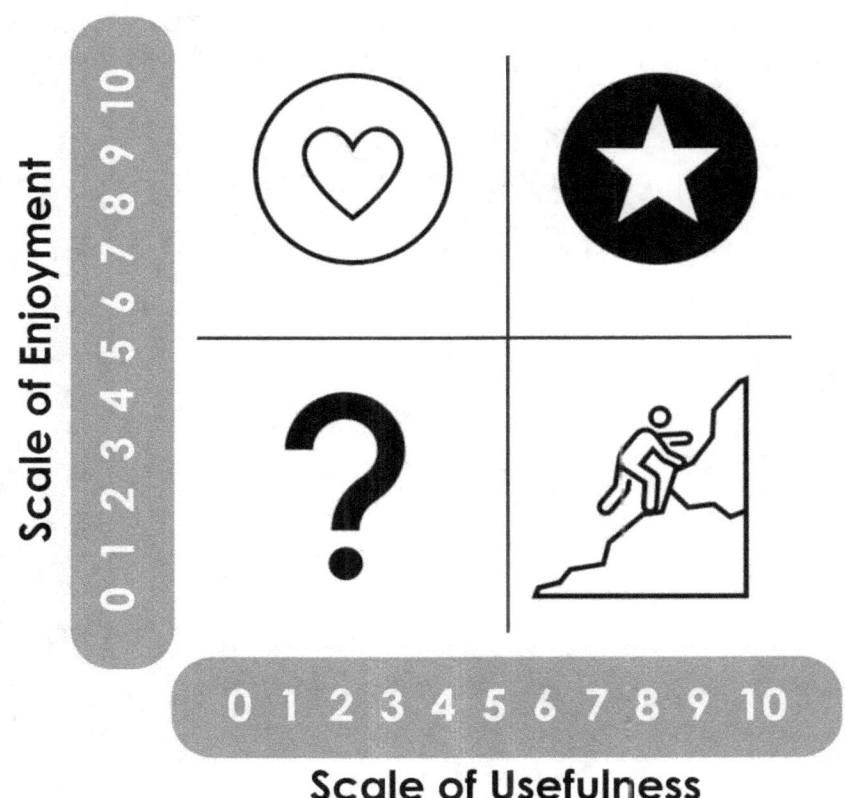

Where do you spend most of your time?

Are there any things you might want to change?
What things might you do less of to enable you to do more of the things you want to do?

How might you make the things you do more enjoyable or useful?

More About Me

Use the space below to represent yourself in words and pictures.
There is no right or wrong and you don't need to share.

Perhaps write a poem.
Or collect images and stick them here.
Get creative and have fun!

Gratefulness Log

It can be helpful to start or end a day TH!NKing about what we are grateful for.

Try making a list of the things that you are grateful for. Keep adding to it whenever you TH!NK of something...

People In My Life

Imagine YOU are in the centre of this circle. TH!NK about your key relationships with the people around you. The closer they are to the centre of the circle, the closer they are to YOU. To the LEFT add the not so good relationships and to the RIGHT add the ones that are good for you.

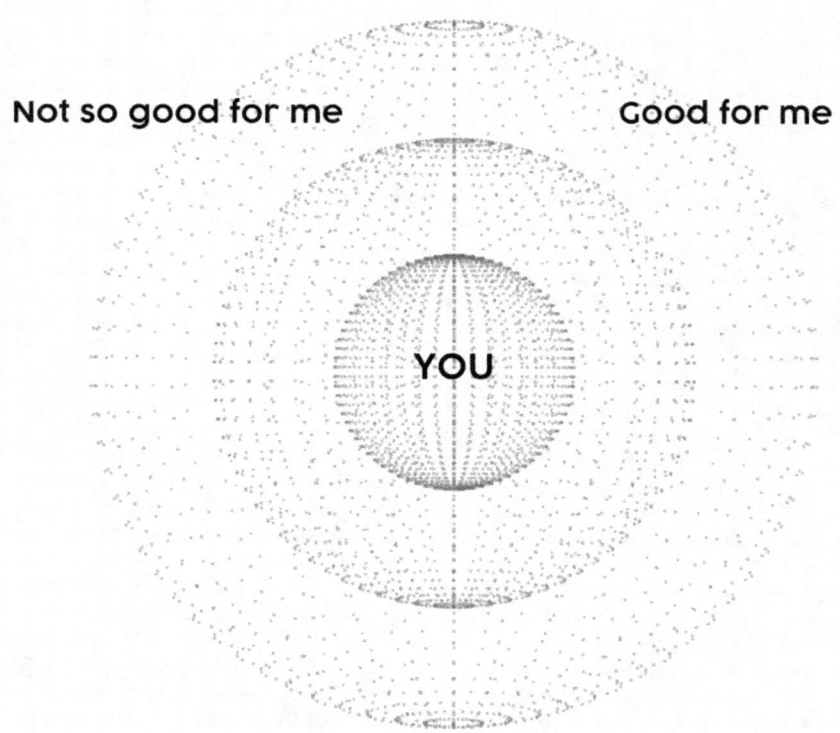

Not so good for me   **Good for me**

YOU

Have a TH!NK about each of these relationships and ask...
What are the positives?
What are the minuses or negatives?
What is interesting?
What about other people - what is their point of view?

Letters From Me

If you could write a letter to anyone that ever existed, who might it be?

How could they possibly help you on your journey?

What questions might you ask them?

Perhaps you could write a letter to your PAST SELF. What advice might you give? What might you take away from this?

What if you wrote a letter to your FUTURE SELF, what might you say?

NOTES

"What would you do in this time, if you truly believed in yourself and those around you?" Jon Alexander

Hindering Thoughts

Thoughts we TH!NK and SAY about ourselves or our situation that don't help us - are Hindering Thoughts.

Do you have any Hindering Thoughts? - we invite you to note them here!

My Hindering Thoughts

1.

2.

3.

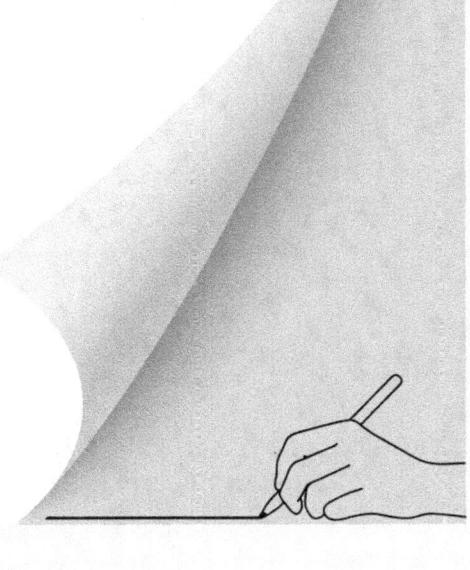

Stuck?

If you want to change your Hindering Thoughts, you can use these four words to move your TH!NKing to somewhere more Helpful. Ask yourself...

What Could I...

...That's More Helpful?

Who else might find this useful?
Try out the What Could I Bird on the next page!

What Could I Bird

The What Could I Bird can help you change your Hindering Thoughts - you just need a square of paper. Follow the instructions below.

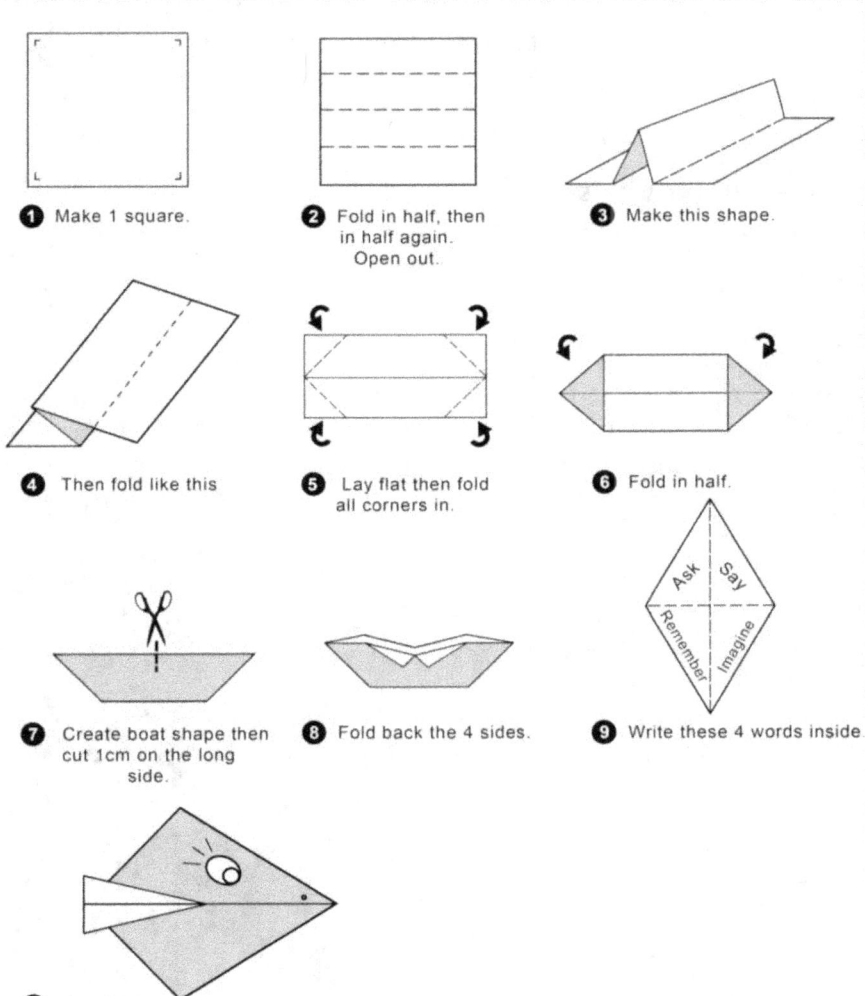

1. Make 1 square.
2. Fold in half, then in half again. Open out.
3. Make this shape.
4. Then fold like this.
5. Lay flat then fold all corners in.
6. Fold in half.
7. Create boat shape then cut 1cm on the long side.
8. Fold back the 4 sides.
9. Write these 4 words inside. (Ask, Say, Remember, Imagine)
10. Decorate.

Helpful Thoughts

With your What Could I Bird to hand, turn your Hindering Thoughts into more Helpful ones.

What Could I...SAY, ASK, REMEMBER, IMAGINE that's more helpful than what I am currently TH!NKing?

My Helpful Thoughts

1.

2.

3.

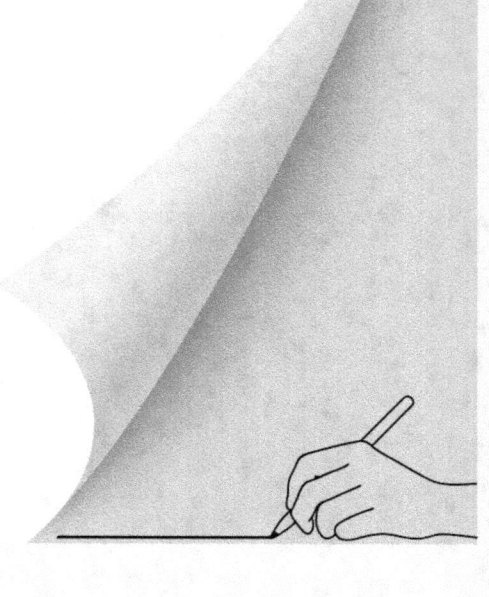

Feelings Check In

Emotions play an important role in our health and happiness. How are you feeling right now? Use the faces below to draw your own feelings. The prompts beneath might help.

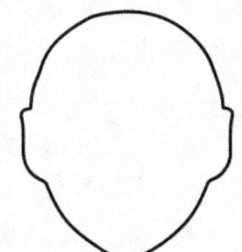 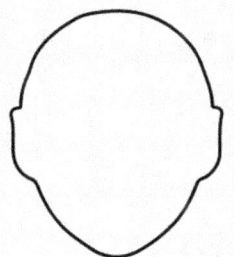 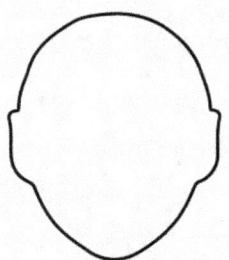

Which emotion might be most helpful right now?

Excited	Relaxed	Happy	Sad	Worried	Scared

Calm	Hopeful	Angry	Nervous	Bored	Tired

Grateful	Joyous	Thoughtful	Amazed	In Love	Proud

Confused	Anxious	Frustrated	Guilty	Hungry	Peaceful

Reasons Why

TH!NK about where you are on the scales. Are you where you want to be? What might you do about that?

How much are you planning for this journey to be useful to you?

How much are you planning to do something outside of your comfort zone? What might that be?

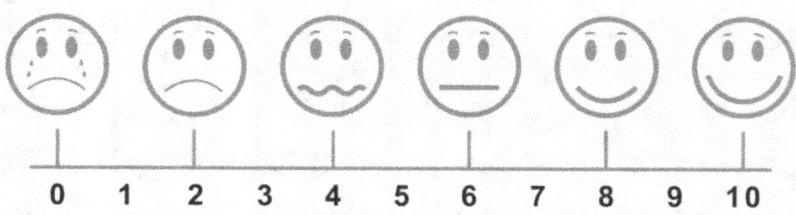

How much do you plan to help others? What might that look like?

My Life

This page is about connecting with what really matters to you.

Imagine you are looking back at your life - you are 99 and have achieved everything you wanted to do. You've had a great life!

What does your life look like?

TH!NK about...
How might you feel?
What are people around you saying?
What did you achieve and how did you achieve it?
How will people remember you?

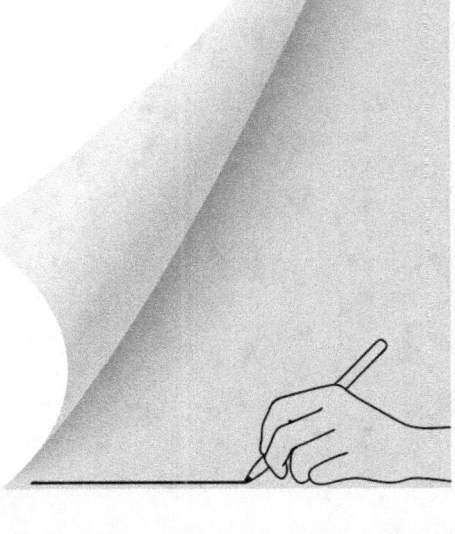

The Good Life

What does YOUR "Good Life" look like? - what brings joy to you, in any aspect of your life? At home, at work, at play, as a family member, carer, colleague, friend, neighbour.

What might you want your "Good Life" to look like?

NOTES

"You are braver than you believe, stronger than you seem and smarter than you think."
A.A Milne

CHAPTER TWO

STRENGTHS AND SKILLS

Strengths and Skills

Understand your own Skills and Strengths and identify your Top Skills

Learn about connecting with others and Gift Conversations

Try Community Asset Bingo and discover the assets (gifts) around you

Find out what Community Connections are important to you

Consider Importance and Control

TH!NK about where to Make a Difference

Reflect on your Good Life

Ask yourself - What Do You Want To Do?

And don't forget to Celebrate!

NOTES

"One might say that human societies have two boundaries. One boundary is drawn by the requirements of the natural world and the other by the collective imagination"
Susan Griffin

Strengths and Skills

Let's TH!NK about YOUR strengths & skills! There are 100 skills captions on the next few pages. For each skill caption tick one of the following options.

I CAN   WE CAN   WE CAN'T BUT KNOW SOMEONE THAT CAN   WE CAN'T AND WE DON'T KNOW ANYBODY THAT CAN

How many skills do you TH!NK YOU will have in each of the above categories? Note your estimates below.

/100   /100   /100   /100

When you have ticked off the skills captions on the next few pages, return here an add up your results.

/100   /100   /100   /100

How different were your results to your predictions?

Tick your skills and add up the totals (25 skills per page).

- Act in a play
- Tell stories
- Care for someone who is ill
- Care for older people
- Care for pets
- Visit a new neighbour
- Care for babies and children
- Volunteering
- Recycle
- Gifting/charitable giving
- Be patient
- Helping others out
- Organise things
- Manage money
- Keep records / fill out forms
- Plan work for others
- Run a stall at a fair or market
- Plan a project or event
- Write a report
- Apply for a job / grant / licence
- Have attention to detail
- Give directions / instructions
- Campaign for a cause
- Take messages
- Speak in public

Tick your skills and add up the totals (25 skills per page).

- Keep promises
- Take responsibility for actions
- Be reliable
- Have a positive attitude
- Be fair
- Keep calm in a crisis
- Stand up for what is right
- Be trusted
- Be honest
- Be self motivated
- Have determination
- Get jobs done
- Give appropriate advice
- Dance like no one is watching
- Sing
- Create sculptures
- Start a business
- Willingness to share
- Be authentic
- See strength in others
- Persuade people to do stuff
- Communicate with others
- Interview people
- Teach computer skills
- Support people to do stuff

Tick your skills and add up the totals (25 skills per page).

👍 👍👎 👍👎 👎👎

- Build things
- Demolish things
- Draw a map
- Grow things
- Be confident using digital things
- Have gardening skills
- Be a peacemaker
- Know lots of people
- Put people at ease
- Connect with people
- Be empathetic
- Be enthusiastic
- Run a social media page
- Coach others
- Start a club
- Waiting
- Be imaginative
- Have a sense of humour
- Spacial reasoning
- Try new things
- Play a musical instrument
- Draw and paint
- Play
- Make up games and stories
- Listen to understand others

Tick your skills and add up the totals (25 skills per page).

- Be physically active
- Use hand tools
- Sort things out
- Cook
- Drive a vehicle
- Make and serve tea
- Clean
- Sew or knit
- Do outdoor activities
- Do sports
- Spot opportunities
- See the bigger picture
- Be able to break things down
- Consider consequences
- Understand risks
- Have lots of ideas
- TH!NK before acting
- Understand other peoples views
- Ask good questions
- Find solutions
- Do hairdressing
- Design games on computers
- Make things
- Repair or mend things
- Send and receive emails

My Top Skills

Looking at the skills you have identified in the last activity - make a note of the ones you TH!NK are most useful to you.

How do you feel?
Use the blank faces below to draw how you feel! Refer back to the Feelings Check In page to help you.

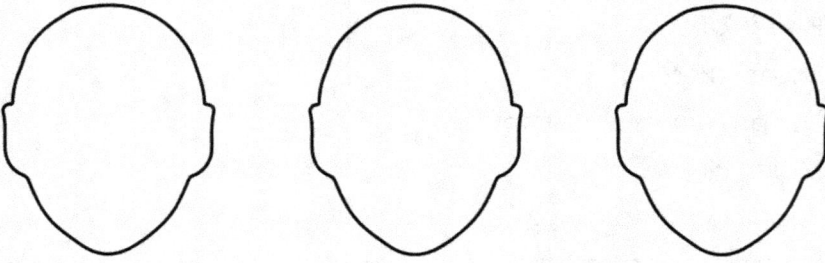

What Else?

TH!NKing about the 100 skills captions - what else might you possibly add?

It can sometimes be hard to identify our own skills.

TH!NK Head, Heart & Hands.

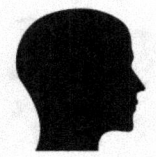

Gifts of the Head - acquiring and sharing knowledge; history, books, art etc

Gifts of the Heart - things that cannot be bought; empathy, volunteering, listening, caring for others, friendship, solidarity etc

Gifts of the Hands - an acquired skill; gardening, walking, stamp collecting, quilting, arts and crafts, fishing etc

Here are some prompts to help you;

Does your skill involve others?
What might a friend say your skills are?
Is your skill completely unique?
Is it a practical skill e.g. an activity or sport?
Is it an emotional skill e.g. empathy?
Is it a mental skill e.g. goal setting?

NOTES

"Act as if what you do makes a difference. It does."
William James

Inspiration

"The ones that are crazy enough to TH!NK they can change the world, are the ones that do!" Steve Jobs

"People might forget what you said or did but they won't forget how you made them feel." Maya Angelou

"Just because somebody has given you a label, it doesn't mean you have to wear it." Deana Bamford

"Go at the speed of trust." Stephen Covey

"Accept the things you cannot change, have courage to change the things you can and the wisdom to know the difference." Serenity Prayer

"Build on what's strong, not on what's wrong." Cormac Russell

Add your own inspirational quote;

— 66 ——————————

——————————  —

Gift Conversations

Gifts are qualities with potential.

Do you know the gifts of those around you; colleagues, friends, family, neighbours and those in your community?
We are not used to talking about what we are good at and the gifts of those around us often go unnoticed.

How might you find you out about the gifts of others and connect with those around you?

Here are some prompts to help with starting a conversation about gifts, recognising the strengths and skills in others;

- What contributions do you like to make to others?

- What do you like doing that makes you forget time?

- What gives you the greatest joy?

- What might your greatest accomplishment of the future be?

- What do you care most about to take action?

- Where in the community do you think you might make a contribution / share one of your gifts?

Who might your next conversation be with?

Community Asset Bingo

We all live in communities that have an impact on us and we all have an impact on our community. TH!NK about what's in YOUR community and take the Challenge - look at the images below and note some of the Assets in YOUR community.
See if you can get a full house!

If you can and feel able to, visit your community and see what else you can find.

Community Connections

Draw yourself in the centre of this circle. Add people, spaces and places that are IMPORTANT to you in the surrounding circles to create a map. Use the things you have identified from the Community Asset Bingo activity on the previous page.

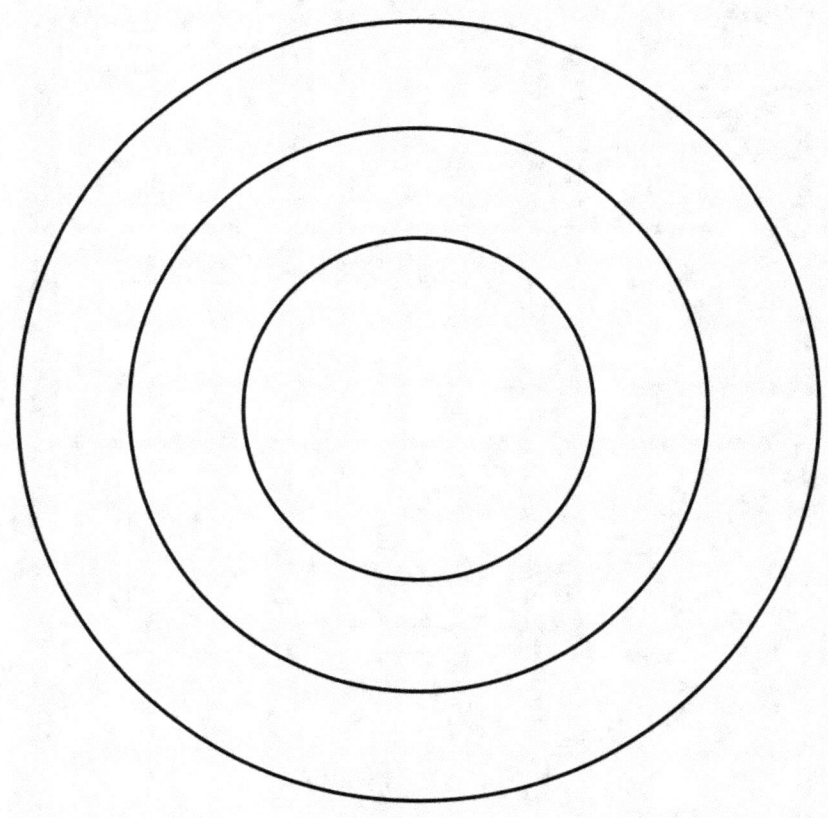

What do you care about the most?

NOTES

"Community is a verb not a noun."
Cormac Russell

Importance & Control

We all have thoughts and concerns, areas of our lives that we wish to be different. It's easy to get overwhelmed or stuck on where to focus.

Understanding what's IMPORTANT to us and what we can CONTROL and therefore act on, is a great place to focus.

On the next page, group your concerns by using the matrix to identify what's important to you AND what influence and control you have.

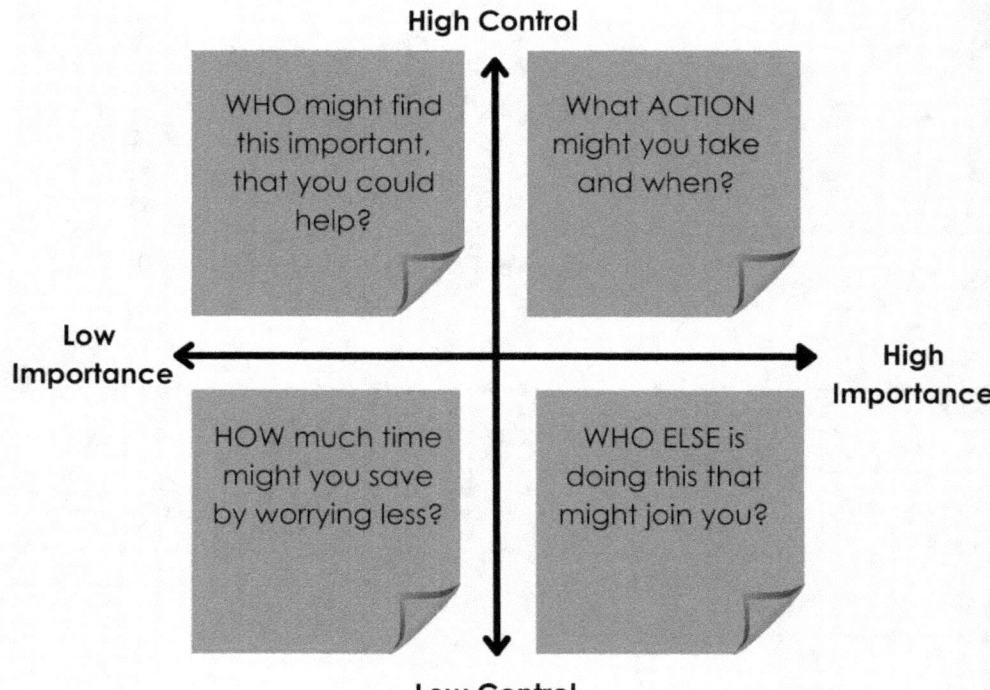

Have a TH!NK and write down your thoughts below.

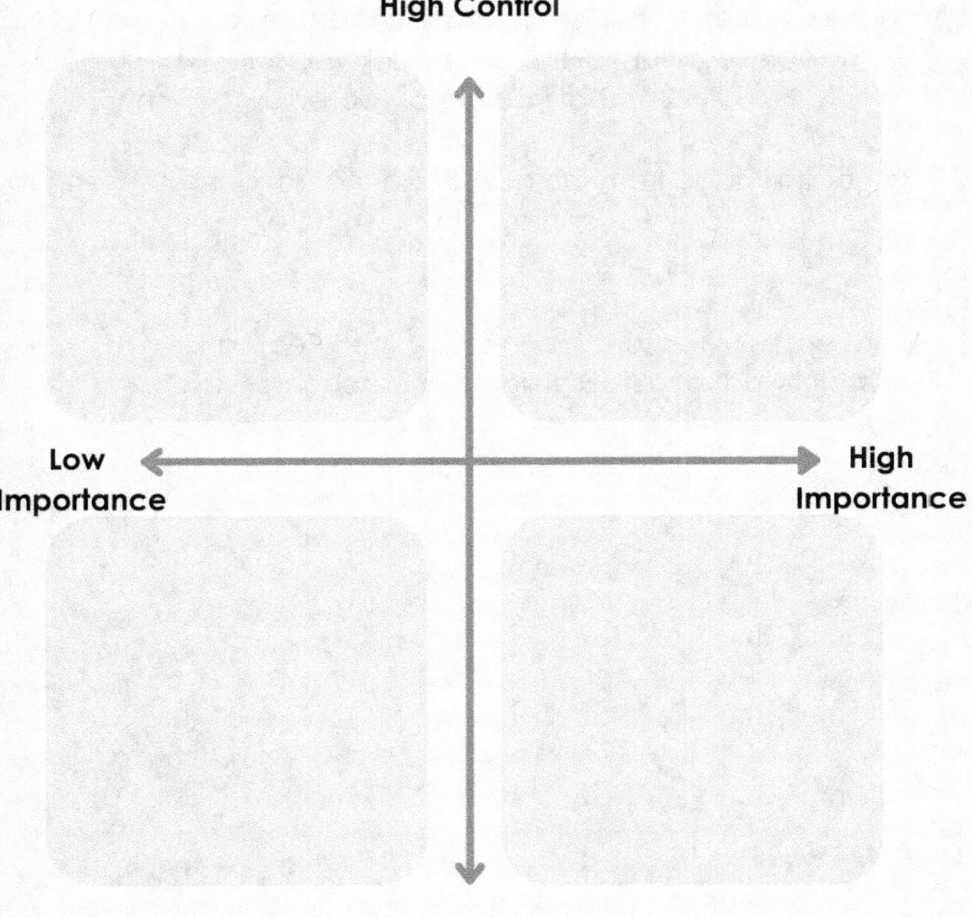

Remember, don't underestimate your ability to to have an INFLUENCE. Even if you think have limited control in a situation - you CAN make a difference!

Making A Difference

Another way of considering what's important to you is to TH!NK about lots of potential topics and ask yourself - What is it you CARE ABOUT that you are prepared to ACT on?

Select an image from the next page that means something to you - or draw your own here.

What are your reasons for choosing this? Keep asking yourself "what else?". Highlight your strongest reason.

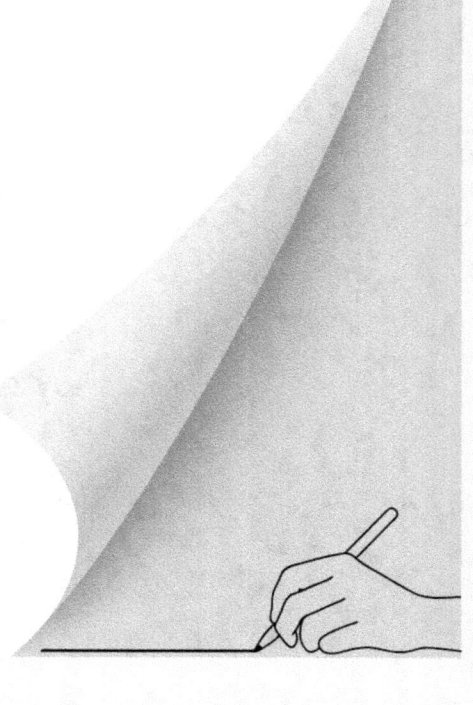

Mental Health

Babies

Myself

Young People

Democracy

Homelessness

People with Disabilities

Children in Care

Refugees

My Family

Humanity

Natural Environment

Older Adults

My Community

The Good Life

TH!NKing back to what your "Good Life" looks like (see Chapter 1 - All About Me) - lets "check in / reflect".

TH!NK about a role in your life; at home, at work, at play, as a family member, carer, colleague, friend, neighbour.

Scoring out of 10 - Where are you now? /10
List the positive reasons you gave this score? What else?

Scoring out of 10 - Where do you want to be?
What does this look and feel like?

/10

Action
What steps might you take to achieve this?
What will you do next?

What Do You Want To Do?

45

Use this space to TH!NK about the things you might want to TAKE ACTION on.

Look over the notes you have made in your journal so far to remind you What's Important to you and where you might want to Make A Difference.

In Section 3 you will find plenty of tools to help you achieve your goals.

Celebrate!

When you have achieved something, however small - CELEBRATE!

Recognising our achievements increases our self belief and in turn motivates us towards achieving our bigger goals. It also helps us to feel good - involve others and share the celebration.

How might you celebrate?

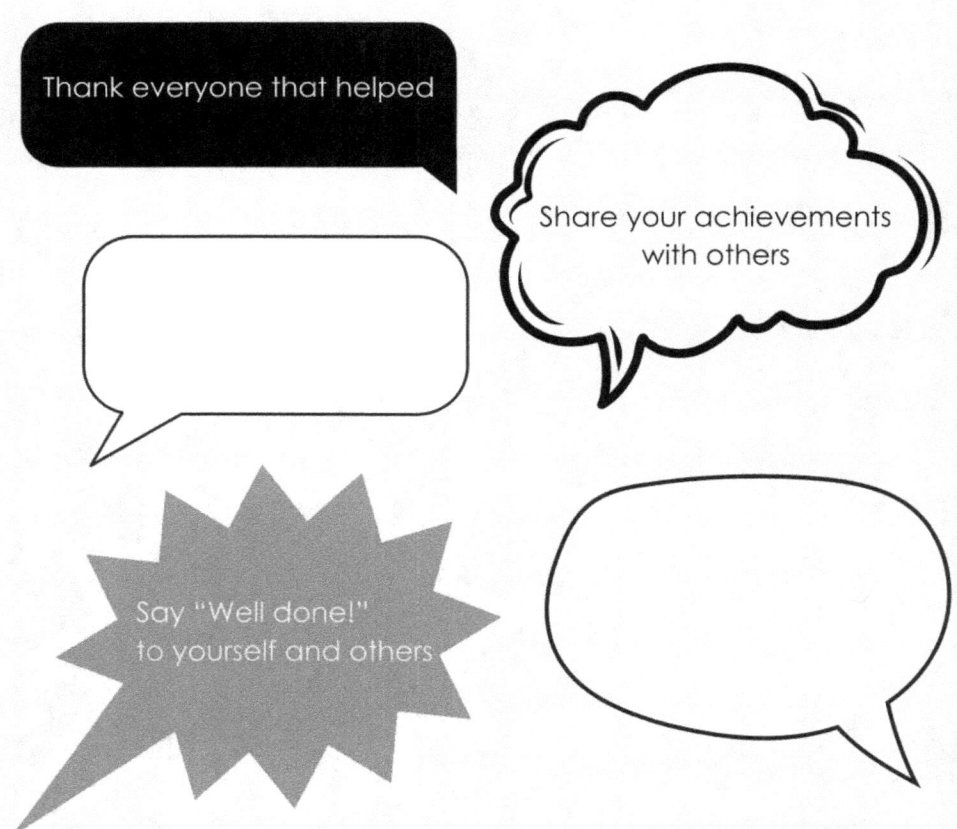

Thank everyone that helped

Share your achievements with others

Say "Well done!" to yourself and others

NOTES

"You are never too old to set a new goal or dream a new dream."
C.S.Lewis

CHAPTER THREE

GOAL SETTING AND TAKING ACTION

Goal Setting & Taking Action

Reset with the Daily Spiral

Manifest ideas with Possibility TH!NKing

Evaluate with P.M.I. and the Internal Triangle

Plan your project with the Elephant Story

Break down your tasks with Umbrella Goals

Involve Others and consider Other Peoples Views

Create a Plan of Action and Imagine Success

Figure out your 4N's and try on the 8 TH!NKing Caps

Celebrate & Reflect!

NOTES

"It is not joy that makes us grateful. It is gratitude that makes us joyful."
David Steindl-Rast

Daily Spiral

You are invited to continue the spiral below, keep it tight and slow. Breathe in for a count of 3 and breathe out for 5 whilst you are spiralling. Keep going for 2 minutes. Play music if that helps.

Then, sarting in the top left, complete the sentences.

This is a great way to start your day or when you need to reset.

I'm Proud of...

I'm Grateful for...

Today I Will...

My Big Dream is...

Possibility TH!NKing

You are invited to try some possibility TH!NKing!

1. TH!NK about something you want some IDEAS for!
Perhaps its a challenge or issue, maybe its something you noted at the end of Chapter 2 that you want to do?

> What is it that I'm looking for ideas for?...

2. Using the wheel, turn this into a High Quality Question.

> How might I possibly... / What could I...?

3. Using the table on the next page write down as many ideas to answer your High Quality Question, as you can.

Use the Creative Prompts on the following pages to help. You'll get over the obvious, through the silly and then to the outrageous...to help you TH!NK. Keep going, there are no wrong answers, it's just getting us TH!NKing.

4. Highlight the answers you want to explore further and select one that you want to ACT ON!

1	
2	
3	
4	
5	
6	
7	
8	
9	
10	
11	
12	
13	
14	
15	

Who else might have fun with Possibility TH!NKing?

Creative Prompts

What might the worlds greatest expert say?	What might (insert person) do?	Imagine you could go forward in time...	Imagine you were a fly on the wall...
Imagine you had the power to...	What might be the easiest solution?	What might be the most outrageous solution?	How might you simplify things?
What might the worlds worst look like?	What might the opposite look like?	How might you achieve your goal quicker?	What could you do today to move things forward?
Turn a problem statement into a helpful solution?	What could I possibly...?	How could I possibly...?	Who could I possibly...?

Use the creative prompts if you get stuck to help you TH!NK of ideas. Often the first ideas we come up with are not our best ones. Only when we do a bit of Possibility TH!NKing can we let go, so the really good ideas come out.

Imagine you could view the situation from a great height	If you could wave a magic wand, what would you wish for?	What could you possibly create?	What could you possibly make disappear?
What if there were no constraints?	What if you had to find a solution?	What if you did have the ability to...?	What possible things might not work?
How could (insert) possibly help?	What could you do to improve your knowledge?	How could you gain the skills needed?	Who in the world could you involve?
What public pledge could you possibly make?	How might you do things faster?	What immediate action could you take right now?	Who else? How else? What else?

PMI

One way to TH!NK about which idea to choose is to use a PMI and consider the Pluses, Minuses and what's Interesting. Try spending a couple minutes on each below. This tool is great for evaluating the outcome of something or making decisions too.

Plus	**Minus**	**Interesting**
		Try asking...
		What if...?
		Perhaps...?
		Could I...?
		Might we...?
		I wonder...?
		How about...?
		Maybe...?
		Who might...?
		How might we possibly...?
		What if we looked at it this way...?
Upsides	Downsides	Alternatively we
Positives	Negatives	could...?

NOTES

"Every single person has capabilities, abilities and gifts. Living a good life depends on whether those capabilities can be used, abilities expressed and gifts given."
John P. Kretzmann and John L. McKnight

Internal Triangle

This is a great opportunity to check in with yourself, your goal and your belief in SUCCESS. Use the next two pages to TH!NK about...

1. YOUR GOAL

WHAT is it that you want to achieve? Be specific.
HOW will you know you have achieved it? What evidence will there be?
WHEN will you have achieved it by? Give a date and time.
HOW will you celebrate?

2. REASON WHY

Write down your reasons why. Keep going asking WHY ELSE? WHAT ELSE? Decide which is your strongest reason.

3. SELF BELIEF

Ask yourself on a scale of 1-10 "How confident am I that I will achieve this goal?"

Have a play with your own Internal Triangle.

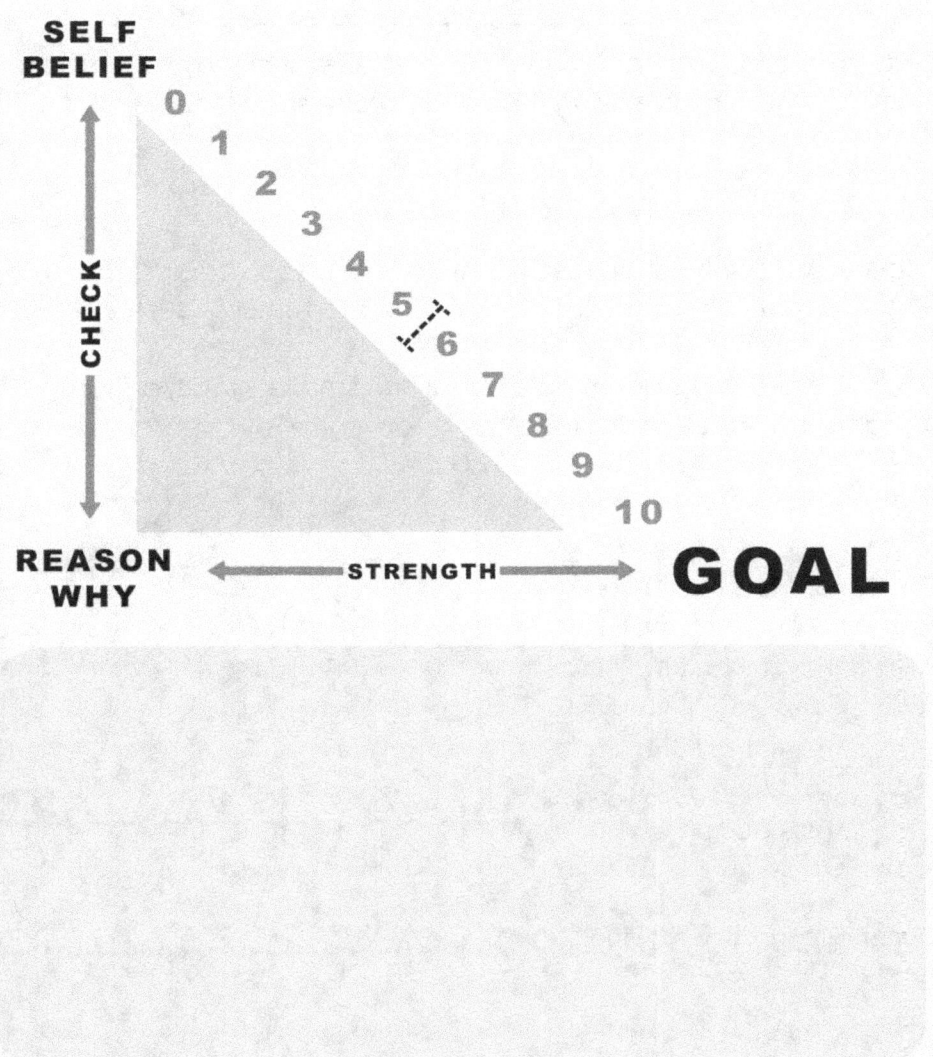

Is your SELF BELIEF 6 or above? - if yes, great! If its less than 5, how might you increase your self belief?
Is your REASON WHY strong enough?
Is your GOAL too big? Could you give yourself more time?
Or break it down to something smaller?

Umbrella Goals

The Umbrella Goal tool is a simple and effective way to plan a big goal by breaking it down into bite sized chunks.

1. Start with your BIG GOAL.

2. Break down your BIG GOAL into smaller goals/topics. The idea is that all the smaller goals add up to the BIG GOAL.

3. Keep breaking down each goal into smaller goals/actions (each row should add up to the goals in the row above).

This is your BIG GOAL - say WHAT it is and WHEN you will achieve it by

Does this row add up to your BIG GOAL?

Does this row added together equal the row above?

Repeat as needed

What ELSE?

Your turn....

TOP TIP - try using post it notes. Your goals/actions are easy to move around!

What ACTION will you take today?

The Elephant Story

This planning tool uses a story to help TH!NK about all the things needed to successfully achieve your goals.

TASKS

RESOURCES

ASSUMPTIONS

Starting with Tasks, work clockwise around the story. Go round more than once and note down your TH!NKing as you go.

OVERCOME AND MINIMISE

RISKS

Refer back to your GOAL.

Have you asked yourself WHAT? Have you said WHEN?
HOW will you know when you've achieved it?
How will you CELEBRATE?

**REASONS
(TO INVOLVE OTHERS)**

**PEOPLE TO
INVOLVE**

Keep a list of the Tasks and Resources you need to prioritise, to help create an Action Plan.

**COMMUNICATE
YOUR GOAL**

OBSTACLES

GAINING BUY IN

Involving Others

What reasons are there to Involve Others? Have a TH!NK about who you might involve and what reasons they might have for helping you. Not sure who to involve? Try using the Involving Others prompts on the next page.

Use the spaces below to note down your thoughts.

What reasons are there to help others?	Who might you involve?	What are their reasons for helping you?
Keep TH!NKing - What else?	Who else - In the whole wide world?	Keep asking - What else?

Involving Others Prompts

Who might have space?	Who has experience?	Is it a family member? Or friend?	Maybe its someone with different skills?
Do they have control?	Is it their job?	Do they have ideas?	Do they have knowledge?
Maybe they share your values?	Someone with connections?	A person that will listen?	Someone creative?
Someone with time?	Do they have followers?	Is it someone helpful?	Who else?

NOTES

"Mix with people who are not like you."
Camerados

Other People's Views

Spending some time TH!NKing about Other People's Views (OPVs) can really help us to solve problems, reach agreements and get things done.

The Perspective Hat is a simple and powerful tool to help TH!NK about Other People's Views.

1. MAKE a Perspective Hat. It's so easy.
2. TH!NK about who it might represent.
3. WRITE or DRAW the name of the person/people on the hat.
4. PRETEND you are them by wearing the hat and TH!NK about things from the other persons perspective.

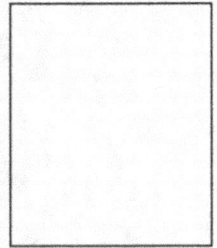

1. Take an A4 piece of paper.

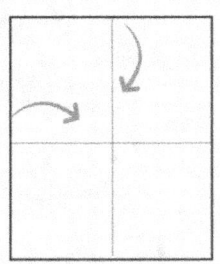

2. Fold in half and half again. Open out.

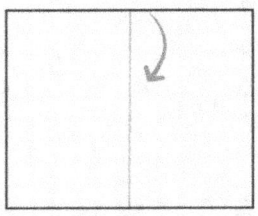

3. Fold in half along the short edge. Keep the folded edge at the top.

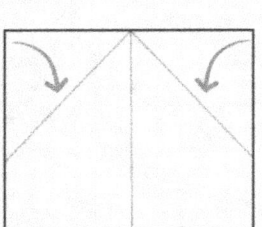

4. Fold the top two corners down to the centre, creating a point.

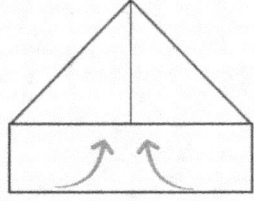

5. On each side fold the bottom flap up and over to make the rim.

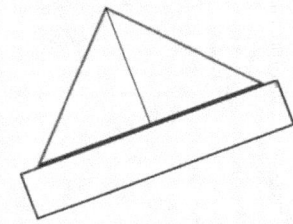

6. Use the hats for lots of things!

Plan of Action

You have had a TH!NK about your goals, what you might need to achieve them and who you might involve - you are ready for an Action Plan.

What will you do?	Date & Times	How will you celebrate?
List your actions	When will you achieve each task?	Who else might you involve?

Imagining Success

Another way of TH!NKing about it. Imagine you have already achieved your goal - TH!NK about how you did it.

This is known as "deconstructing success".

Try TH!NKing about these questions...

What TASKS did you do?

What RESOURCES did you need?

What REASONS did you have to INVOLVE OTHERS?

WHO did you involve?

How did you let them know about what you wanted them to DO?

How did you COMMUNICATE your ideas?

How did you gain their BUY IN? What was in it for them?

What OBSTACLES did you face? How did you OVERCOME them?

What RISKS were there? How did you MINIMISE them?

Did you make any ASSUMPTIONS? How did this affect what happened?

The 4N Chart

The 4N Chart is a simple and powerful tool to encourage open and healthy relationships. It can help to understand where you can get most benefits with least effort.

It can be used at the start of a new group or new project and to review existing teams or work.

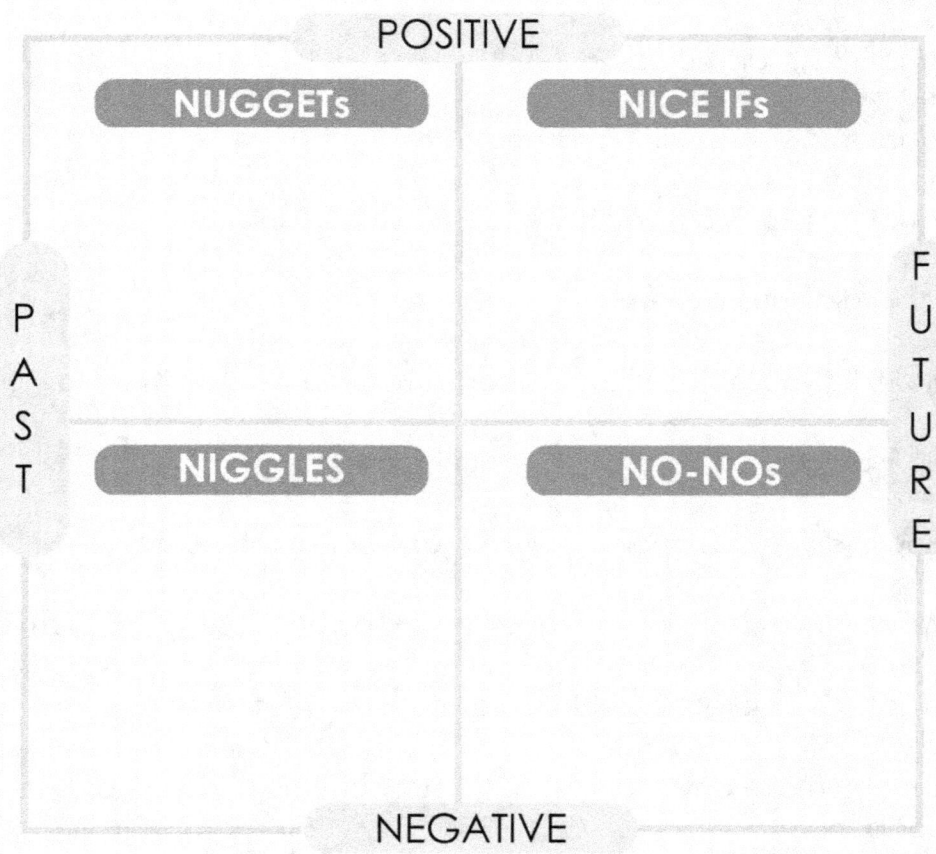

Starting in the top left - focus on the positive actions / behaviours; what works well. The NUGGETS. We are not used to spending time on the positives, often taking them for granted. Ask "what else?" a number of times, there are often more NUGGETS than we first see.

Move to the bottom left - focus on the negative actions / behaviours. The NIGGLES. Work backwards and ask yourself "why?" several times, until you feel you have found the real cause of the negative actions / behaviours.

Go to the bottom right - these are the negative actions / behaviours you want to put a stop to. The NO-NOs. TH!NK about their root cause and how they could be avoided.

Finish in the top right - TH!NK about those positive actions / behaviours that you would like more of. The NICE-IFS. What might you need to have more of these? Ask "how I can have more of these?"

The 8 TH!NKing Caps

The 8 TH!NKing Caps is an excellent tool to create FOCUS and support decision making.

BLUE CAP - COORDINATE
Decides WHAT TH!NKing is needed and WHEN

WHITE CAP - EVIDENCE
Focuses on the FACTS and TRUTH

RED CAP - FEELINGS
Describes the FEELINGS about the situation

BLACK CAP - CAUTION
TH!NK about the DOWNSIDES?

YELLOW CAP - UPSIDES
TH!NK about the POSITIVES

GREEN CAP - POSSIBILITY
Ideas, fresh TH!NKING and solutions

PURPLE CAP - CONNECT
Who WITH and WHEN will I share?

GOLD CAP - ACTION
What will I DO?

With an understanding of the 8 TH!NKing Caps their colours and meanings, use the NAVIGATION TOOL below to help direct your TH!NKing. Start in the centre with COORDINATE and choose where you want to go next.

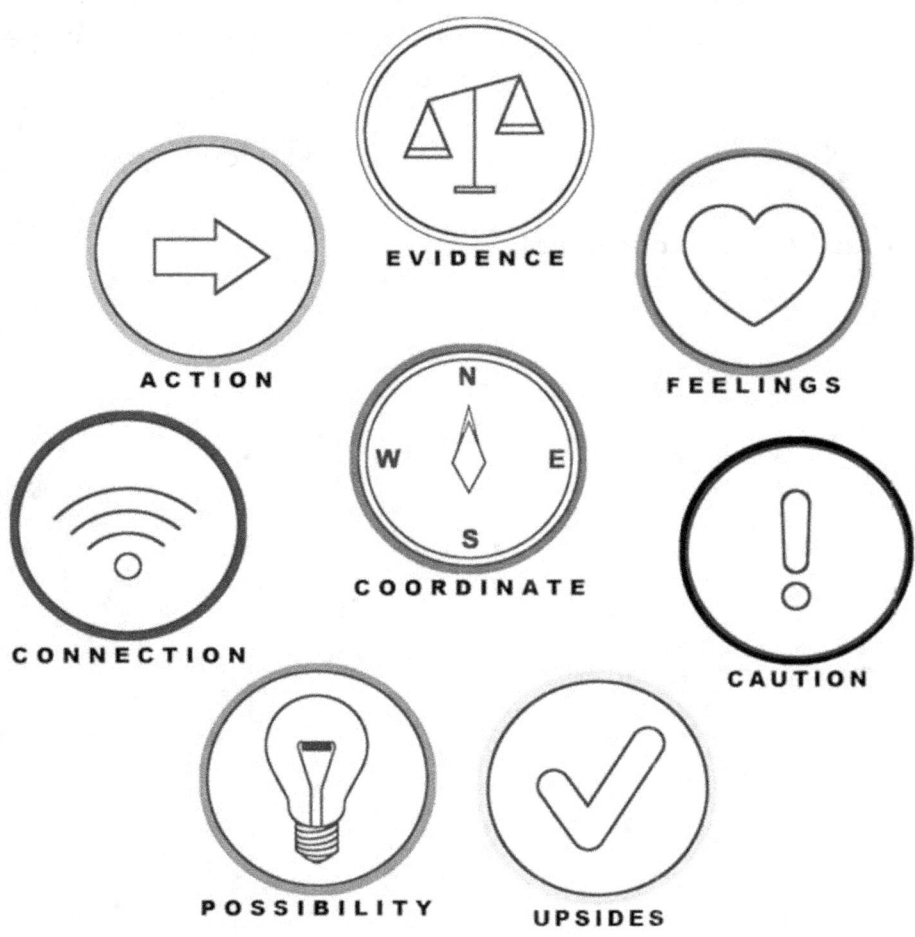

Top Tip - it may help to direct your final thoughts to ACTION

Celebrate!

Don't forget to celebrate your achievements and successes!

Recognizing our achievements fosters joy, strengthens social connections and offers a valuable opportunity to acknowledge the efforts on our journey.

Don't forget to include others and share the celebrations!

What have you achieved?

How will you celebrate?

Reflections

75

TH!NK and ask your self some questions about your experiences and learnings whilst using this Journal.

What did I learn that was new to me?

What insights did this new knowledge give to me?

Try out the PMI Tool to explore the Pluses, Minuses and see what was Interesting!

What will you do next?

NOTES

"All of us are smarter than any of us."
Jon Alexander

TOOLS TO TH!NK

Here's a list of the Tools shared in this Journal. We hope you find them useful.

You can find more on our website; www.thinkfc.org.uk

Chapter 1 ALL ABOUT ME	Chapter 2 STRENGTHS & SKILLS	Chapter 3 SETTING GOALS & TAKING ACTION
Your Story Your Time More About Me Gratefulness Log People in My Life Letters From Me Hindering Thoughts Stuck? What Could I Bird Helpful Thoughts Feelings Check In Reasons Why My Life The Good Life	Strengths & Skills My Top Skills What Else? Gift Conversations Community Asset Bingo Community Connections Importance & Control Making a Difference The Good Life What Do You Want to Do? Celebrate	Daily Spiral Possibility Th!nking PMI Internal Triangle Umbrella Goals Elephant Story Involving Others OPVs Plan of Action Imagine Success 4N Tool 8 Th!nking Caps Celebrate Reflections

If you aren't sure which tool to use and when, check out our FLOW CHART (on the next page) to help direct you!

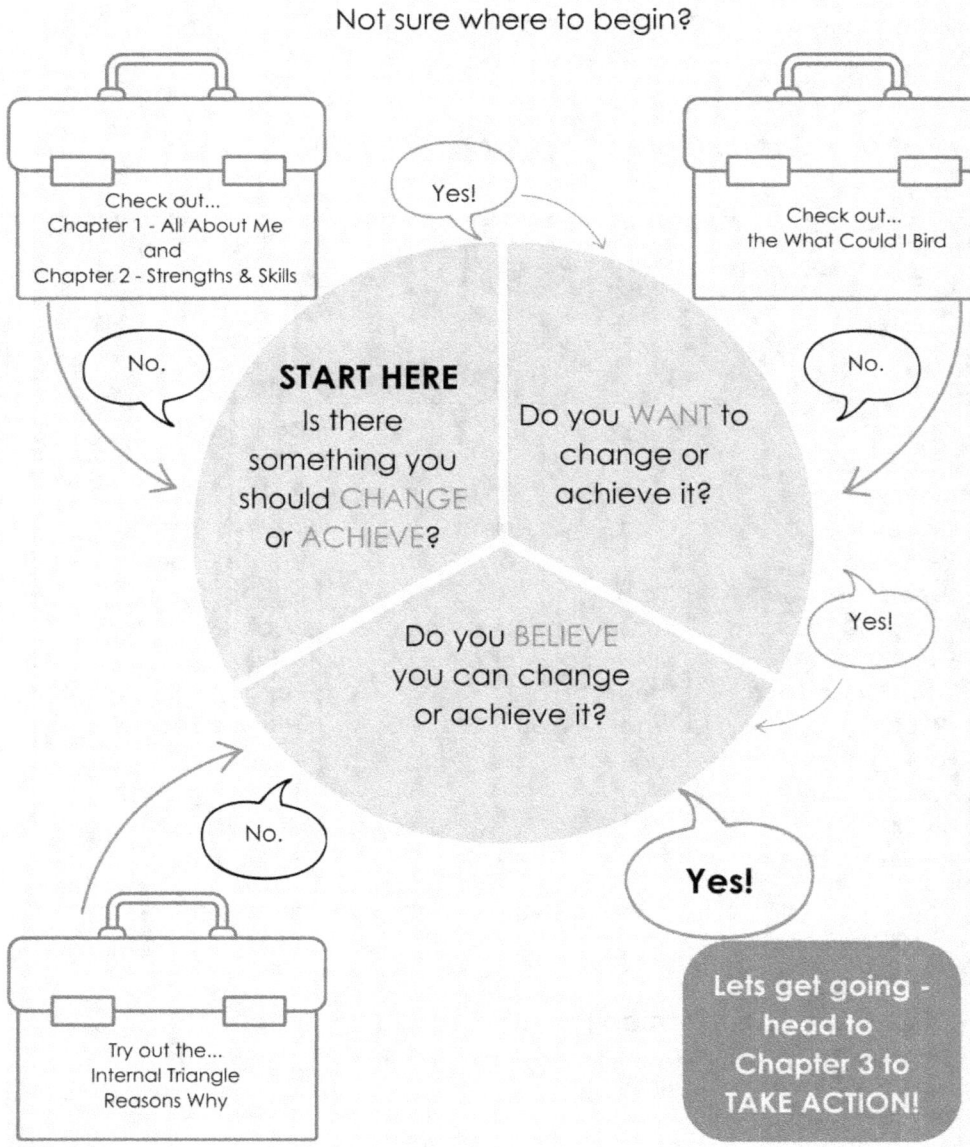

Not sure which tools to use?
Check out our Tool Boxes to help you navigate...

I want to reset
Daily Spiral
Gratefulness Log

I feel overwhelmed
Feelings Check In
Importance & Control

I want help with my Hindering Thoughts
Hindering Thoughts
Stuck?
What Could I Bird
Helpful Thoughts

I want to discover my gifts
Strengths & Skills
My Top Skills
What Else?

I want to connect with others
Gift Conversations
Community Asset Bingo
Community Connections

I want to consider my future
Your Story
More About Me
My Life
The Good Life

I'm not sure what to act on
Making a Difference
What Do You Want to Do?

I want to solve a problem with new ideas
Possibility TH!NKing
Involving Others
OPVs

I want to take action
Internal Triangle
The Elephant Story
Umbrella Goals
Plan of Action

I want to focus and support decision making
Daily Spiral
8 TH!NKing Caps
Imagining Success
4N Tool

I want help to review something
4N Tool
PMI

I want to celebrate
Celebrate
Reflections

TH!NK FC
• Authentic • Connect • Trust

We hope you've enjoyed Your Journal and are TH!NKing differently! Please feel free to share the ideas and tools you've found with others and if you have any questions about the journal or the tools, you can email us at any time. We'd love to hear from you - let us know what you think about the Journal, your stories, what actions you have taken etc!

You can reach us by email;
Deana@thinkfc.org.uk / Ian@thinkfc.org.uk / Helen@thinkfc.org.uk

Inspired by our friends

Cormac Russell
Go Mad Thinking
Edward De Bono Foundation
Liberating Structures

Thank you to everyone for your support to make this journal happen with particular gratitude to Ian Wilson, Deana Bamford & Helen Bazen for content and design - made in Canva.

Find more tools and resources to use and share at www.thinkfc.org.uk or use this QR Code

Working with TH!NK FC

Would you like YOUR OWN version of the Journal? This white label edition can be tailored to you and your organisation! Send us an email to get the ball rolling...

TH!NK FC runs a variety of COURSES, TASTER DAYS and SUMMITS.

CONNECT : LISTEN : SHARE : COLLABORATE : ACTION

With an array of TH!NKing tools and engaging activities we can help you find your own solutions to challenges and bring people together - join us in this journey to Level the Playing Field. Contact us today to see how we might support you...

Find our BOOKS at Coalville C.A.N Makers Shop or online;

Watch this space for more...

www.thinkfc.org.uk

NOTES

"The journey of a thousand miles begins with one small step."
Lao Tzu

NOTES

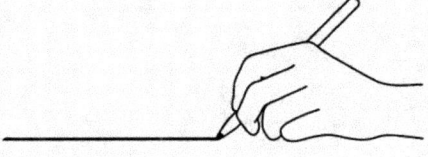

NOTES

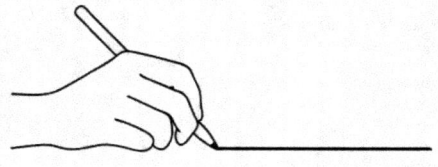

www.ingramcontent.com/pod-product-compliance
Lightning Source LLC
Chambersburg PA
CBHW071220070526
44584CB00019B/3091